FRUITS & VEGETABLES

FRUITS & VEGETABLES

Poems

by

Erica Jong

HOLT, RINEHART AND WINSTON
New York   Chicago   San Francisco

FIRST EDITION

The following poems were first published in *Poetry:*
"Touch"; "Narcissus, Photographer"; "Books";
"Where It Begins." "The Heidelberg Landlady" first
appeared in *The Beloit Poetry Journal* as "The
Landlady," and has been slightly revised. Parts of
"Fruits & Vegetables" and "The Objective Woman" first
appeared in *Twen* (West Germany) in German
translation.

Other poems were previously published in the
following periodicals: *Aphra, Intro, #3, The Beloit
Poetry Journal, Mademoiselle,* and *The Southern Review.*

Special thanks to Grace Darling.

*Grateful acknowledgment is made for use of the
following:*

One line from "First Meditation," © 1955 by
Theodore Roethke, from *The Collected Poems
of Theodore Roethke.* Reprinted by permission of
Doubleday & Company, Inc.

One line from "Blue" by Rafael Alberti from *The
Poems of Rafael Alberti,* translated by Mark Strand.
Reprinted by permission of Las Americas Publishing
Company of New York City.

One line from *The African Boy* by Elizabeth Sargent,
© 1963 by The Macmillan Company. Reprinted by
permission of The Macmillan Company.

Three lines from "Test" by Nicanor Parra from *Poems
and Antipoems,* translated by Miller Williams, © 1967
by Nicanor Parra. Reprinted by permission of New
Directions Publishing Corporation.

Contents

FRUITS & VEGETABLES 1

TOUCH

Seven 13

With Silk 15

The Sheets 16

The Quarrel 18

Downward 19

Touch 20

His Silence 22

The Ecological Apocalypse
as Foretold to
Adam & Eve 23

The Man Under the Bed 24

HERE COMES

Arse Poetica 27

The Teacher 29

Walking Through the Upper East Side 31

Digging the Chinese Cemetery 33

Here Comes 34

Fracture 36

Two More Scenes from the Lives
of the Vegetables 38

Cheese 40

THE OBJECTIVE WOMAN

The Commandments 43
Aging 45
Bitter Pills for the Dark Ladies 47
The Objective Woman 49

FLOWER EATERS

The Man Giving Birth in the Dark 57
Living In 58
In Sylvia Plath Country 60
A Reading 63
Imaginary Landscapes 64
The Saturday Market 66
The Heidelberg Landlady 69
Student Revolution 71
Flying You Home 73
Narcissus, Photographer 78
Flower Eaters 79
You Operate 81
Books 82
The Book 83
Where It Begins 85

"*Poetry, the creative act, the archetypal
sexual act. Sexuality is poetry. . . .
Petrarch says that he invented the beautiful
name of Laura, but that in reality Laura
was nothing but the poetic laurel which
he had pursued with incessant labor.*"

         *   *   *

"*We must eat again of the tree of knowledge
in order to fall into innocence.*"
—Norman O. Brown

FRUITS & VEGETABLES

> *"It is hard to imagine a civilization without onions."*
> —*Julia Child*

> *"Only weggebobbles and fruit. . .*
> *I wouldn't be surprised if it was*
> *that kind of food you see produces*
> *the like waves of the brain the*
> *poetical."*
> —*James Joyce*

> *"In recent decades there has been a*
> *distinct falling off in the interest*
> *shown in hunger artists."*
> —*Franz Kafka*

> *"Know me come eat with me."*
> —*James Joyce*

Goodbye, he waved, entering the apple.
That red siren,
whose white flesh turns brown
with prolonged exposure to air,
opened her perfect cheeks to receive him.
She took him in.
The garden revolved
in her glossy patinas of skin.
Goodbye.

2

O note the two round holes in onion.

3

Did I tell you about
my mother's avocado?
She grew it from a pit.
Secretly, slowly in the dark,
it put out grub-white roots
which filled a jelly jar.
From this unlikely start,
an avocado tree with bark
& dark green leaves
shaded the green silk couch
which shaded me

throughout my shady adolescence.
There, beneath that tree
my skirt gave birth to hands!
Oh memorable hands of boys
with blacked-out eyes
like culprits
in the *National Enquirer*.
My mother nursed that tree
like all her children,
turned it around so often
towards the sun
that its trunk grew twisted
as an old riverbed,
& despite its gaudy leaves
it never bore
fruit.

4

Cantaloupes: the setting sun at Paestum
slashed by rosy columns.

5

I am thinking of the onion again, with its two O mouths,
like the gaping holes in nobody. Of the outer skin, pinkish
brown, peeled to reveal a greenish sphere, bald as a dead
planet, glib as glass, & an odor almost animal. I consider
its ability to draw tears, its capacity for self-scrutiny,
flaying itself away, layer on layer, in search of its heart
which is simply another region of skin, but deeper &

greener. I remember Peer Gynt; I consider its sometimes double heart. Then I think of despair when the onion searches its soul & finds only its various skins; & I think of the dried tuft of roots leading nowhere & the parched umbilicus, lopped off in the garden. Not self-righteous like the proletarian potato, nor a siren like the apple. No show-off like the banana. But a modest, self-effacing vegetable, questioning, introspective, peeling itself away, or merely radiating halos like lake ripples. I consider it the eternal outsider, the middle child, the sad analysand of the vegetable kingdom. Glorified only in France (otherwise silent sustainer of soups & stews), unloved for itself alone—no wonder it draws our tears! Then I think again how the outer peel resembles paper, how soul & skin merge into one, how each peeling strips bare a heart which in turn turns skin. . .

6

A poet in a world without onions,
in a world without apples
regards the earth as a great fruit.

Far off, galaxies glitter like currants.
The whole edible universe drops
to his watering mouth. . .

Think of generations of mystics
salivating for the fruit of god,
of poets yearning to inhabit apples,
of the sea, that dark fruit,
closing much more quickly than a wound,

5

of the nameless galaxies of astronomers,
hoping that the cosmos will ripen
& their eyes will become tongues. . .

7

For the taste of the fruit
is the tongue's dream,
& the apple's red
is the passion of the eye.

8

If a woman wants to be a poet,
she must dwell in the house of the tomato.

9

It is not an emptiness,
the fruit between your legs,
but the long hall of history,
& dreams are coming down the hall
by moonlight.

10

They push up through the loam
like lips of mushrooms.

(Artichoke, after Child): Holding the heart base up, rotate it slowly with your left hand against the blade of a knife held firmly in your right hand to remove all pieces of ambition & expose the pale surface of the heart. Frequently rub the cut portions with gall. Drop each heart as it is finished into acidulated water. The choke can be removed after cooking.

12

(Artichoke, after Neruda)

It is green at the artichoke heart,
but remember the times
you flayed
leaf after leaf,
hoarding the pale silver paste
behind the fortresses of your teeth,
tonguing the vinaigrette,
only to find the husk of a worm
at the artichoke heart?
The palate reels like a wronged lover.
Was all that sweetness counterfeit?
Must you vomit back
world after vegetable world
for the sake of one worm
in the green garden of the heart?

But the poem about bananas has not yet been written. Southerners worry a lot about bananas. Their skin. And nearly everyone worries about the size of bananas, as if that had anything to do with flavor. Small bananas are sometimes quite sweet. But bananas are like poets: they only want to be told how great they are. Green bananas want to be told they're ripe. According to Freud, girls envy bananas. In America chocolate syrup & whipped cream have been known to enhance the flavor of bananas. This is called a *banana split*.

14

The rice is pregnant.
It swells past its old transparency.
Hard, translucent worlds inside the grains
open like fans. It is raining rice!
The peasants stand under oiled
rice paper umbrellas cheering.

Someone is scattering rice from the sky!
Chopper blades mash the clouds.
The sky browns like cheese soufflé.
Rice grains puff & pop open.

"What have we done to deserve this?"
the peasants cry. Even the babies
are cheering. Cheers slide from their lips
like spittle. Old men kick their clogs

into the air & run in the rice paddies
barefoot. This is a monsoon! A wedding!

Each grain has a tiny invisible parachute.
Each grain is a rain drop.

"They have sent us rice!" the mothers scream,
opening their throats to the smoke. . .

15

Here should be a picture of my favorite apple.
It is also a nude & bottle.
It is also a landscape.
There are no such things as still lives.

16

In general, modern poetry requires (underline one):
a) more fruit; b) less fruit; c) more vegetables; d) less
vegetables; e) all of the above; f) none of the above.

17

Astonishment of apples. Every fall.
But only Italians are into grapes,
calling them eggs.
O my eggs,
branching off my family tree,
my father used to pluck you,

leaving bare twigs on the dining room table,
leaving mother furious on the dining room table:
picked clean.
Bare ruined choirs
where late the sweet.
A pile of pits.

18

Adam naming the fruit
after the creation of fruit,
his tongue tickling
the crimson lips of the pomegranate,
the tip of his penis licking
the cheeks of the peach,
quince petals in his hair,
his blue arms full of plums,
his legs wrapped around watermelons,
dandling pumpkins on his fatherly knees,
tomatoes heaped around him in red pyramids. . .

                    peach
                    peach
                    peach
                    peach
                    peach

                              he sighs

to kingdom come.

TOUCH

"The spirit moves, but not always upward."
—*Theodore Roethke*

Seven

The 7 mysterious holes in the body

        :

          the sacredness of 7
          depends on these

The 5 holes in the head

     :

      the Moloch of the mouth
      & gluttony the 5th of deadly sins
      the ears O stop them
      the 2 roads of the nostrils
      leading to Rome

But the eyes are not holes
; they are scars
remains of a time
when the whole body was eye
& light flowed everywhere
like sperm

       The 7 mysterious holes
       do not include

         :

          the navel,
          that link
          with a vegetable world,
          that green vine
          rooting toward earth

;
but the anus loves
poetry
& is prolific

      & the hole in the penis
      sings to the cunt

            :

             of the pyramids of Egypt
             & the hanging gardens of Babylon
             & the 7th day of Creation

There is, for example, the 7th heaven of the Mohammedans
& the 7th circle of hell, moated with blood

There is Dante climbing down the caves of flesh
There are the 7 hills
the 7 seas

With Silk

A girl with silk pockets
& eyes slipperier than fish
was waiting if she ever let him go—
her Chinese lover
with balls
like fresh lichees
& tongue on her tongue
like a kumquat.
At night
he entered the body
of her dream,
his black hair
massed on his forehead,
his tennis trophies ranged
in barriers around them,
his long legs leaping
towards love
or some ground stroke.
His body was white
in the dream light,
his penis dark
as a tree.
She would never know
who the other was,
waiting,
speaking her high-pitched Mandarin
like wind chimes,
trilling syllables
he never understood,
binding & unbinding her feet
as if they were hearts.
She sits
on a grass mat
scented with jasmine,
her hands mannered
as an old scroll painting,
her eyes fishing.
They hook on his
while he makes love to her.
A syllable of moonlight
shatters
on the floor.

The Sheets

We used to meet
on this corner
in the same wind.
It fought us up the hill
to your house,
blew us in the door.
The elevator rose
on gusts of stale air
fed on ancient dinners.
Your room smelled
of roach spray and roses.

In those days
we went to bed with Marvell.
The wind ruffled sheets and pages,
spoke to us through walls.
For hours I used to lie
with my ear to your bare chest,
listening for the sea.

Now the wind is tearing
the building down.
The sheets are rising.

They billow through the air like sails.

White with your semen,
holding invisible prints
of the people we were,

the people we might have been,
they sail across the country
disguised as clouds.

Momentarily they snag
on the Rocky Mountains,
then rise
shredded into streamers.

Now they are bannering westward
over California
where your existence
is rumored.

The Quarrel

It is a rainy night
when the wind beats at your door
like a man you have turned away

He comes back trailing leaves & branches
He comes back in a shower of earth
He comes back with blades of grass
still clinging to his hair

No matter how hard he holds you
he is still elsewhere
making love to another

No matter how hard you hold him
you are still
elsewhere

Your bodies slide together
like wet grass blades
You cling & stop the raindrops
with your tongues

Later you rise
& pick the nettles from your hair
You take the leaves for clothing

Your loneliness
is a small gray hole in the rain
You rise & go knocking
at his locked front door

Downward

Because your eyes are the color of shadows on Chartres Cathedral
  because your sunglasses are smoke
    because smoke curls out of your ears to music
      because your mustache shades the letters of your words
       because your neck is planted in your shoulders
        because your tiny nipples rise to meet my tongue
         because the navel of your earth has never been discovered by
        because we are going downward   Columbus

    Because the black hair whorls on your belly
      because your knees are mountain ranges
       because my mouth is a valley of melting snow
        because your penis is no metaphor
         because your thighs are horses galloping
          because your feet are the beginning & the beginning
          because their soles tattoo the air   again
           because we are going we are going downward

Touch

A man in armor,
a huge plume
shooting from his head,
velvet buckles at his hips,
joints of oiled steel
moving with the sound
of taffeta,
comes to my room
late at night.

His face is visored.
His chest
is emblazoned with crowns.
A fine tattoo of gold
blooms on his arms.

Through a chink in the visor
I see what may be an eye,
or perhaps the reflection
of its loss.

His codpiece gleams like a knife.

I think myself naked,
my skin white

as the cut side of a pear.
I think he will slash me.

But when we move
our bodies together
we make such noises. . .

It has been this way for years.
Our steel hands clasp.
Our legs lock into place
like coupling freight trains.

His Silence

He still wears the glass skin of childhood.
Under his hands, the stones turn mirrors.
His eyes are knives.

Who froze the ground to his feet?
Who locked his mouth into an horizon?
Why does the sun set when we touch?

I look for the lines between the silences.
He looks only for the silences.

Cram this page under his tongue.
Open him as if for surgery.
Let the red knife love slide in.

The Ecological Apocalypse
as Foretold to Adam & Eve

Because he dreams of seeding the world with words
his eyes bite
She looks   He looks away
He is snowblind
from staring at her breasts
They make love
This is marked by asterisks
those gaps
disguised as stars

    *   *   *

He thinks the future is a mouth
She invites him
into her apple

The Man Under the Bed

The man under the bed
The man who has been there for years waiting
The man who waits for my floating bare foot
The man who is silent as dustballs riding the darkness
The man whose breath is the breathing of small white
                                        butterflies
The man whose breathing I hear when I pick up the phone
The man in the mirror whose breath blackens silver
The boneman in closets who rattles the mothballs
The man at the end of the end of the line

I met him tonight   I always meet him
He stands in the amber air of a bar
When the shrimp curl like beckoning fingers
& ride through the air on their toothpick skewers
When the ice cracks & I am about to fall through
he arranges his face around its hollows
he opens his pupilless eyes at me
For years he has waited to drag me down
& now he tells me
he has only waited to take me home
We waltz through the street like death & the maiden
We float through the wall of the wall of my room

If he's my dream he will fold back into my body
His breath writes letters of mist on the glass of my cheeks
I wrap myself around him like the darkness
I breathe into his mouth
& make him real

HERE COMES

"What is anti-poetry?

* * *

A woman with her legs open?

* * *

A jet-propelled coffin?"
    —Nicanor Parra

Arse Poetica

for Leonard & Patricia

I

Item: the poet has to feed himself & fuck himself.

II

Salt the metaphors. Set them breast up over the vegetables
& baste them with the juice in the casserole. Lay a piece
of aluminum foil over the poem, cover the casserole &
heat it on top of the stove until you hear the images
sizzling. Then place the poem in the middle of a rack in
the preheated oven.

Roast for an hour & twenty minutes, regulating heat so
that poem is always making quiet cooking noises. The
poem is done when drumsticks move in their sockets &
the last drops of juice drained from the vent run clear.
Remove to a serving dish & discard trussing.

III

Once the penis has been introduced into the poem, the
poet lets herself down until she is sitting on the muse
with her legs outside him. He need not make any motions
at all. The poet sits upright & raises & lowers her body
rhythmically until the last line is attained. She may pause
in her movements & may also move her pelvis & abdomen
forward & back or sideways, or with a circular corkscrew
motion. This method yields exceptionally acute images

& is, indeed, often recommended as yielding the summit of aesthetic enjoyment. Penetration is at its deepest. Conception, however, is less apt than with other attitudes.

This position is also suitable when the muse is tired or lacking in vigor since the poet plays the active role. Penetration is deepest when the poet's body makes an angle of 45 degrees with the muse's. A half-erect muse will remain in position when this attitude is adopted since he cannot slip out of the poem.

The Teacher

The teacher stands before the class.
She's talking of Chaucer.
But the students aren't hungry for Chaucer.
They want to devour her.
They are eating her knees, her toes, her breasts, her eyes
& spitting out
her words.
What do they want with words?
They want a real lesson!

She is naked before them.
Psalms are written on her thighs.
When she walks, sonnets divide
into octaves & sestets.
Couplets fall into place
when her fingers nervously toy
with the chalk.

But the words don't clothe her.
No amount of poetry can save her now.
There's no volume big enough to hide in.
No unabridged Webster, no OED.

The students aren't dumb.
They want a lesson.
Once they might have taken life
by the scruff of its neck

in a neat couplet.
But now
they need blood.

They have left Chaucer alone
& have eaten the teacher.

She's gone now.
Nothing remains
but a page of print.
She's past our helping.
Perhaps she's part of her students.
(Don't ask how.)

Eat this poem.

Walking Through the Upper East Side

All over the district, on leather couches
& brocade couches, on daybeds
& "professional divans," they are confessing.
The air is thick with it,
the ears of the analysts must be sticky.

Words fill the air above couches & hover there
hanging like smog. I imagine
impossible Steinberg scrolls,
unutterable sounds suspended in inked curlicues
while the Braque print & the innocuous Utrillo
look on look on look on.

My six analysts, for example—

the sly Czech who tucked his shoelaces
under the tongues of his shoes,
the mistress of social work with orange hair,
the famous old German who said:
"You sink, zerefore you are,"
the bouncy American who loved to talk dirty,
the bitchy widow of a famous theoretician,
& another—or was it two?—I have forgotten—

they rise like a Greek chorus in my dreams.
They reproach me for my messy life.
They do not offer to refund my money.

& the others—siblings for an hour or so—
ghosts whom I brushed in & out of the door.
Sometimes the couch was warm from their bodies.
Only our coats knew each other,
rubbing shoulders in the dark closet.

Digging the Chinese Cemetery
(near the grave of my grandfather-in-law)

The Chinese Christian Burial Association
has grouped politely on the shores
of the new world.

The members softly call the roll
so as not to wake
the sleepwalkers.

America is here beneath these elms.
The Chinese Christian Burial Association
is about to enter it.

Pon Fung Chen Lee Moy
Wong Tong Tsien Tsang Chew
Chang Chan Jong Long Song. . . .

The Chinese Christian Burial Association
is digging
home.

Here Comes

(a flip through *Bride's*)

The silver spoons
were warbling
their absurd musical names
when, drawing back
her veil (illusion),

she stepped into
the valentine-shaped bathtub,
& slid her perfect bubbles
in between
the perfect bubbles.

Oh brilliantly complex as
compound interest,
her diamond gleams
(Forever) on the edge
of a weddingcake-shaped bed.

What happens there
is merely icing since
a snakepit of dismembered
douchebag coils (all writhing)
awaits her on the tackier back pages.

Dearly beloved, let's hymn
her (& Daddy) down
the aisle with

epithalamions composed
for Ovulen ads:

"It's the right
of every (married) couple
to wait   to space   to wait"
—& antistrophes
appended by the Pope.

Good Grief—the groom!
Has she (or we)
entirely forgot?
She'll dream him whole.
American type with ushers

halfbacks headaches drawbacks backaches
& borrowed suit
stuffed in a borrowed face
(or was it the reverse?)
Oh well. Here's he:

part coy pajamas,
part mothered underwear
& of course
an enormous prick
full of money.

Fracture

This constant ache
is my leg's message to me.
"Hello. Hello. Hello.
You're getting there," it says,
"step by step."

Legs aren't stars
which sputter out
& go on gleaming anyway.
I've lived, of course,
with phantom limbs

but this fracture
doesn't point to
amputation. No.
It hisses something
much more final.

Skin lantern,
necklace of teeth,
the bones & sinews
are in revolt against us.
We keep them down

with little bribes:
vitamins, penicillin,
& now these pounds of plaster,
but they will bury us,
good bolsheviks,

& know it.
So they've got time to bide.
Meanwhile: spread-eagled
on these crutches, a cripple
sucking the ground with rubber

nipples, or else a knight,
up to my ass in armor,
I limp & swing my way
across the street
& up the steps,

moving, here & now,
step by step,
towards the future,
that incurable
fracture.

Two More Scenes from the Lives of the Vegetables

"(only the knife knows the heart of the yam)"
—E.N. Sargent

I: Borscht

We entered Russia backwards through the borscht,
paddling our kayak of sour cream,
legs hanging down in the crimson water,
& the banks resounding
with Russian Tea Room Music,
movie scores for *Docteur Z.*

It was a miserable winter in Paris,
all the girls at Le Drugstore wearing Zhivago coats,
& the Hotel Stella turning off the heat
& only cold water in the bidets.

But here in the soup it's cozy.
Your cheeks are ruddy from reflections on the water.
Birches bend over the bowl of the lake.
Chekhov rides up to meet us in a one-horse shay.
Somewhere I think I see a black monk come floating. . .

The waiters all look like Tolstoy's peasants—
except they speak Yiddish.
One gave a violin recital once in Town Hall.

The soup is substantial.
You could almost walk on it as if it were water.
It is biblical, in fact: a red sea.
Look! Someone has written "Yuri loves Lara" in sour cream!

II: Carrot

They dangle the carrot before our eyes.
We walk.
It bounces against the green sky.
Its leaves droop, a wounded parachute.
We have always walked behind it.
Actually we believe the carrot to be
God's penis.
That is why we walk behind it.
It is disappointing, wrinkled and small.
It's the only one we've got.
How we dream of a great carrot to follow!
Blown up like a Macy's balloon on Thanksgiving,
floating over the prismatic static of color T.V.,
it seems to point the way
with a finger so large no one can doubt it.
But our carrot is more dead than alive.
Flies fly in halo formation around it.
Worms peek out, waving goodbye.
Even the dirt will not cling to it.
The root hairs hang down
like the skimpy beards of ancient Chinamen.
We continue to walk behind it.
Someday, they will stop the cart
and let us eat it.
By then it will be cleft with a black valley.
It will hold landscapes, a whole geography of fear.
And by then too, our teeth will have fallen out.
They will strew the road behind us,
breadcrumbs for Hansel & Gretel.

Cheese

Spelunking through the blue caves of the Roquefort
under a golden Gouda moon,
we thought of the breasts of the Virgin
which are also blue. Very few
cheeses are,
and Mary does not belong
in a poem on cheese.
                    Or does She?
We are mice in this wedge
of cheesy poetry, we are about
to be trapped.
                    How peaceful (on the other hand) to be a
                                                      cheese!
To merge with the Great Eater
as every mystic (or mouse)
has some time wished.

Goudas whirl in the sky,
shedding their rinds like prayer wheels;
already the Brie is soft with ecstasy.
Look for that Bel Paese which saints speak of
where the holes dream the Swiss cheese,
where plate and knife exist only in visions,
where milk and cream
are merely memories,
like history,
like Mary.

THE OBJECTIVE WOMAN

*Woman's a long moan of a word
with a man in it. . .*

The Commandments

*"You don't really want to be a poet. First
of all, if you're a woman, you have to be
three times as good as any of the men.
Secondly, you have to fuck everyone. And
thirdly, you have to be dead."*
                    —*a male poet, in conversation*

If a woman wants to be a poet,
    she should sleep near the moon with her face open;
    she should walk through herself studying the landscape;
    she should not write her poems in menstrual blood.

If a woman wants to be a poet,
    she should run backwards circling the volcano;
    she should feel for the movement along her faults;
    she should not get a Ph.D. in seismography.

If a woman wants to be a poet,
    she should not sleep with uncircumcised manuscripts;
    she should not write odes to her abortions;
    she should not make stew of old unicorn meat.

If a woman wants to be a poet,
    she should read French cookbooks and Chinese
                        vegetables;
    she should suck on French poets to freshen her breath;
    she should not masturbate in writing seminars.

If a woman wants to be a poet,
    she should peel back the hair from her eyeballs;

she should listen to the breathing of sleeping men;
she should listen to the spaces between that breathing.

If a woman wants to be a poet,
she should not write her poems with a dildo;
she should pray that her daughters are women;
she should forgive her father for his bravest sperm.

Aging

(balm for a 27th birthday)

Hooked for two years now on wrinkle creams   creams for
crowsfeet   ugly lines (if only there were one!)
any perfumed grease   which promises   youth   beauty
not truth   but all I need on earth
       I've been studying   how women age

            how

it starts around the eyes   so you can tell
a woman of 22 from one of 28 merely by
a faint scribbling near the lids   a subtle crinkle
      a fine line
extending from the fields of vision

            this

in itself is not unbeautiful   promising
      as it often does
insights which clear-eyed 22 has no inkling of
promising   certain sure-thighed things in bed
certain fingers on your spine & lids

            but

it's only the beginning   as ruin proceeds downward
lingering for a while around the mouth   hardening the smile
into prearranged patterns (irreversible!)   writing furrows
from the wings of the nose   (oh nothing much at first
      but "showing promise"   like your early poems

            of deepening)

& plotting lower to the corners of the mouth   drooping them
a little   like the tragic mask   though not at all grotesque
as yet   & then as you sidestep   into the 4th decade
beginning to crease the neck   (just slightly)
                    though the breasts below

                                                    especially

when they're small (like mine) may stay high far
                    into the thirties
still the neck will give you away   & after that the chin
which   though you may snip it back & hike it up under
your earlobes will never quite love your bones as it once did

                                                    though

the belly may be kept firm through numerous pregnancies
by means of sit-ups   jogging   dancing   (think of Russian ballerinas)
                    & the cunt
as far as I know is ageless   possibly immortal   becoming simply
more open   more quick to understand   more dry-eyed than at 22

                                                    which

after all   is what you were dying for   (as you ravaged
islands of turtles   beehives   oysterbeds   the udders of cows)
desperate to censor changes which you simply might have let play
over you   lying back   listening   opening yourself
                    letting the years make love the only way   (poor blunderers)

                                                    they know

Bitter Pills for the Dark Ladies

> *"—hardly a person at all, or a woman,*
> *certainly not another 'poetess,' but. . ."*
> —Robert Lowell about Sylvia Plath

If you've got to   if after trying to
give it up (like smoking or Nembutal)
if after swearing to   shut it up   it keeps on
yakking (that voice in your head)
that insomniac who lives across the wall,
that amateur Hammondist
who plays those broken scales next door
o then   consider yourself doomed to.

Ambition bites. Bite back.
(It's almost useless.) Suppose yourself born
half black, half Jewish in Missis-
sippi, & with one leg
                    You get the Idear?
Jus' remember you got no rights. Anything go wrong
they gonna roun' you up & howl "Poetess!"
(sorta like "Nigra!") then kick the shit outa you
sayin': You got Natural Rhythm (28 days)
so why you wanna mess aroun'?

Words bein' slippery & poetry bein'
mos'ly a matter of balls,
men what gives in to the lilt and lift of words
(o love   o death   o organ tones   o dickey!)
is "Cosmic." You is "Sentimental."
So dance in your Master's bed (or thesis) & shut

yo' mouth. Ain't you happiest there?

If they let you out   it's as Supermansaint
played by S. Poitier   with Ph.D.[2]   & a buttondown fly
washed whiter than any other on the block.
& the ultimate praise is always a question of nots:
>   viz. not like a woman
>   viz. "certainly not another 'poetess' "

meanin'

>   she got a cunt but she don't talk funny
>   & he's a nigger but he don't smell funny

& the only good poetess is a dead.

The Objective Woman

I

For I praise the women of America with their electric purple sunglasses
       & disposable nipples
For I praise their cherryfrost lips & the ivory blizzards
       of their fingernails
For I praise the firmessence of their ultralucence
       & the ultralucence of their firmessence
For I praise their nair & moondrops, their cupid's quiver douches
For I praise their eyewriters & what is written on their eyes
For I praise their bodysmooth clingthings, their curvalon braslips
For I praise their odor of bluegrass, their elusive tigress white shoulders
For I praise their candied brandy toenails which grow longer after death
For I praise their deodorized armpits & their sprayed & powdered crotches
For I praise their electric typewriters which never stop humming
       & the hearts of their men which stop
For I praise their vacuum cleaners which howl with their own voiceless rage
For I praise their electronic answering machines, their plug-in mothers
For I praise young women twisting their wedding bands
       & old women with empty wombs & full shopping bags
For I praise crones with rouged wrinkles who shop in garbage
For I praise all women awaiting repairmen & all women who sleep with bottles
For I praise shopping carts & stirrups & ten-cent rest rooms
For I praise women who buy shoes which hurt & hats which are unreturnable
For I praise their outsides which become their insides
       & their insides which shall become their outsides

II

The Nose

The evidence mounts.
The bottles line up backward
in her mirror.

In each golden hollow floats
an embalmed homunculus.
Ambush.
Enormous dirigible roses
are blooming
in the corners of the room.
They float up
& explode against the ceiling.
Someone is planting orange trees in Versailles
& tending vats of perfume.
There's a tiger yawning in the four-poster
(reading "The Story of O").
On the night table: Tabu, Russian Leather, Vol de Nuit.
"What makes a shy girl get Intimate?"
"There is only one Joy."
& suddenly the gilded cupids
make obscene gestures.
She thinks,
"She looked deep into herself & found nothing."
The mad-eyed violinist is about to seize
the lady pianist.
"Tigress," he growls, "Iced Tigress."
"Toujours Moi," she replies.
The country of the nose.

III

The Rings

After her husband died,
she had his wedding band
soldered to her own.
He was buried bare-handed,
slid into the earth.

Her hands move among the objects
which pretend to be my life.
She wears both rings on one finger.

Was it gold she sought to spare?
Or was she scared
of being married to a dead man?
How were their fingers linked?
Their mouths?
He was buried with his gold teeth on.
Darling, till death do us.

IV

The Dryer

Cleaned & peeled & sealed
down to her fingertips,
unabel to touch
or smell herself,
her capsule stuffed
with thumbed copies
of "Vogue" & "Bazaar,"
her urine siphoned off
into the classified files
of the CIA,
her hair standing
weightlessly on end,
wind whipping
around her helmeted ears,
the first female American astronaut
is being launched!
She rises like Beatrice
into a sky

where all the stars
are Florentine gold.

No love is made
by touch in paradise.
Only the minds meeting
in concentric rings
of wind & bells,
only the legs of the compasses
meshing & turning.
Solitary mute,
always awaiting
the prince for whom
it will be worthwhile
to shake the meteors
out of her hair.
He comes.
He combs her out.
He's gay.

V

OB-GYN

Probing the long poem of her body
where she lies riding,
her knees framing his face,
her breasts & belly tented white,
he looks away
as if forgetting
that his hand
has disappeared.

It's dark.

He chatters about ski resorts.

Does she prefer Kitzbühel to Aspen?

He's touched some tiny town
high in the alps
where the sky sinks its blue teeth
into the mountains
& the sun slides down behind the peaks
like buttered rum.

A light goes on
in the uppermost chalet
above the tree line.
(Your ovaries are fine.)

> Bring light!
> A miner's hat or flashlight.
> Is it like climbing Everest at night?
> One false step empties you back into the sky?
> What do the eyes of the fingertips hook on?
> Skeletons from lost expeditions?
> Babies with the faces of old men?
> The womb blooming, a forest of peonies?

Not applicable.
Your poems are codes.
Pap. BI. CA.
Uptake. Follow-up.

> You look away.

> You tell me how expert you are.

I see that you stay upright
on the surface of the snow.

But I imagine how
the dark core of the mountain
sucks at your dreams
& I see you threading
a black forest
taking the curves gently
knowing it doesn't matter
if you ski through trees
easily looping left & right

Or falling
as if falling asleep
the shudder of your teeth
the spasm of your falling into her
moving through trees at night
moving through branches

Skiers above you
charms on a long bracelet
blue-faced angels
angels in animal fur

trusting the edge
you leave
no footprints

FLOWER EATERS

*"The shadow is bluest when the body
that casts it has vanished."*
—*Rafael Alberti*

The Man Giving Birth in the Dark

The man giving birth in the dark
has died
& come back
to life again,

is stretching out his arms
in the dark
as if to embrace
favorite ghosts.

His heart stops
& starts.
Once more
he has been pardoned

for nothing.
It is my father
making the darkness
into daughters.

Living In

(my grandmother's house)

We entered you like a house,
blowing along
the white curtains.

In the kitchen
with its old aroma of pot roast,
in among the cannisters of tea,
the lavendered closets
with pillowed rows of pink soap,
boxes of cottonwool
& unfinished embroideries,

we said
how we'd like to be lived in
after our death.

Then we began to replace you,
seeping in like cave water,
changing your old order,
defending ourselves
with our own smells.

(I poured espresso
from your teapot,
hung black curtains
in your bathroom.)

Sometimes,
coming home suddenly,
I'd catch you,
your cheek as soft as willow tips,
shaking your head from side to side,
denying
the cancer that was eating you.

I knew
your ghost as my own wish
& wasn't frightened,
but you
refused to stay.

Now, armored by our walls of books,
paintings you wouldn't have approved
& foods you'd never taste,
we find ourselves
alone at last.

Yesterday
we visited your grave.

You were all there.

In Sylvia Plath Country

for Grace

The skin of the sea
has nothing to tell me.

I see her diving down
into herself—

past the bell-shaped jellyfish
who toll for no one—

& meaning to come back.

*

In London, in the damp
of a London morning,
I see her sitting,
folding & unfolding herself,
while the blood
hammers like rain
on her heart's windows.

This is her own country—
the sea, the rain
& death half rhyming
with her father's name.

Obscene monosyllable,
it lingers for a while

on the roof
of the mouth's house.

I stand here
savoring the sound,
like salt.

*

They thought your death
was your last poem:
a black book
with gold-tooled cover
& pages the color of ash.

But I thought different,
knowing how madness
doesn't believe
in metaphor.

When you began to feel
the drift of continents
beneath your feet,
the sea's suck,
& each
atom of the poisoned air,
you lost
the luxury of simile.

Gull calls, broken shells,
the quarried coast.

This is where America ends,
dropping off
to the depths.

Death comes
differently in California.
Marilyn stalled
in celluloid,
the frame stuck,
& the light
burning through.

Bronze to her platinum,
Ondine, Ariel,
finally no one,

what could we tell you
after you dove down into yourself
& were swallowed
by your poems?

A Reading

The old poet
with his face full of lines,
with iambs jumping in his hair like fleas,
with all the revisions of his body
unsaying him,
walks to the podium.

He is about to tell us
how he came to this.

Imaginary Landscapes

for my parents

Who are these small determined figures
              with turbaned heads
                         coming
to doric temples
                   in
                         fifteenth-century galleons
              with
medieval castles
                   in the background?
         They speak
                   & gesture in the halflight,
                              bring
         cattle, parcels
                         to the classic shore
         below the gothic hill.
                     Sunlight moonlight twilight starlight
gleams across
              a stagey sea.
                              Clouds toss. Sails fill.
         Windlessly,
                   what banners wave?
                   Whose landscape
                              is this mind?
Whose bluish breasts became
              these castled hills?
                              Whose darkness is

this winter afternoon?
Whose darkness is
this darkening gallery?
Turn softly mind, wind,
Claude Lorrain,
Turner's making
light of Venice,
showing
his true
colors.

The Saturday Market

for Alexander Mitscherlich

Lumbering down
in the early morning clatter
from farms
where the earth was hard all winter,
the market women bear
grapes blue as the veins
of fair-skinned women,
cherries dark as blood,
roses strewn like carnage
on makeshift altars.
They come
in ancient rattling trucks
which sprout geraniums,
are stained
with strawberries.
Their fingers thick
& thorn-pricked,
their huge smock-pockets
jingling pennies,
they walk,
heavy goddesses,
while the market
blossoms into bleeding
all around them.
Currants which glitter
like Christmas ornaments
are staining

their wooden boxes.
Cherries, grapes—
everything
seems to be bleeding!
I think
how a sentimental
German poet
might have written
that the cut rose
mourns the garden
& the grapes
their Rhineland vineyard
(where the crooked vines
stretch out their arms
like dancers)
for this
is a sentimental country
& Germans
are passionate gardeners
who view with humanity
the blights of roses,
the adversities of vineyards.
But I am not fooled.
This bleeding is, no doubt,
in the beholder's eye,
& if
to tend a garden
is to be civilized,
surely this country
of fat cabbages
& love-lavished geraniums
would please

an eighteenth-century
philosopher.
Two centuries, however,
buzz above my head
like hornets over fruit.
I stuff my mouth with cherries
as I watch
the thorn-pricked fingers
of the market women
lifting & weighing,
weighing, weighing.

The Heidelberg Landlady

Because she lost her father
in the First World War,
her husband in the Second,
we don't dispute
"There's no Gemütlichkeit in America."

We're winning her heart
with filter cigarettes.
Puffing, she says,
"You can't judge a country
by just twelve years."

Gray days,
the wind hobbling down sidestreets,
I'm walking in a thirties photograph,
the prehistoric age
before my birth.

This town was never bombed.
Old ladies still wear funny shoes,
long, seedy furs.
They smell of camphor and camomile,
old photographs.

Nothing much happened here.
A few jewelry shops changed hands.
A brewery. Banks.
The university put up a swastika, took it down.
The students now chant HO CHI MINH & hate Americans

on principle.
Daddy wears a flyer's cap
& never grew old.
He's on the table with the teacakes.
Mother & grandma are widows.

They take care of things.
It rains nearly every day;
every day, they wash the windows.
They cultivate jungles in the front parlors,
lush tropics

framed by lacy white curtains.
They coax the earth with plant food, scrub the leaves.
Each plant shines like a fat child.
They hope for the sun,
living in a Jewless world without men.

Student Revolution
(Heidelberg, 1969)

After the teach-in
we smeared the walls with
our solidarity,
looked left, & saw
Marx among the angels,
singing the blues.

The students march,
I (spectator)
follow.
Here (as everywhere)
the Polizei
are clean, are clean.

In Frankfurt,
the whores lean out
their windows, screaming:
"Get a job—you dirty
hippies!" Or words
(auf Deutsch) to that effect.

I'm also waiting
for the Revolution,
friends.
Surely, my poems
will get better.
Surely, I'll no longer

fear my dreams.
Surely I won't murder
my capitalist father
each night
just to inherit
his love.

Flying You Home

"I only remember the onion, the egg and the boy.
O that was me, said the madman."
—*Nicholas Moore*

I

"I bite into an apple & then get bored
before the second bite," you said.
You were also Samson. I had cut
your hair & locked you up.
Besides, your room was bugged.
A former inmate left his muse
spread-eagled on the picture window.
In the glinting late-day sun
we saw her huge & cross-eyed breasts appear
diamond-etched
against the slums of Harlem.
You tongued your pills & cursed the residents.
You called me Judas.
You forgot I was a girl.

2

Your hands weren't birds. To call
them birds would be too easy
They drew circles around your ideas
& your ideas were sometimes parabolas.
That sudden Sunday you awoke
& found yourself behind the looking glass
your hands perched on the breakfast table

73

waiting for a sign.
I had nothing to tell them.
They conversed with the eggs.

3

We walked.
Your automatic umbrella snapped
into place above your head
like a black halo.
We thought of climbing down rain puddles
as if they were manholes.
You said the reflected buildings
led to hell.
Trees danced for us,
cut-out people turned sideways
& disappeared into their voices.
The cities in our glasses took us in.
You stood on a scale, heard the penny drop—
but the needle was standing still!
It proved that you were God.

4

The elevator opens & reveals me
holding African violets.
An hour later I vanish
into a chasm whose dimensions
are 23 hours.
Tranquilized, brittle
you strut the corridors
among the dapper young psychiatrists,

the girls who weave rugs all day,
unravel them all night,
the obesity cases lost in themselves.
You hum. You say you hate me.
I would like to shake you.
Remember how it happened?
You were standing at the window
speaking about flying.
Your hands flew to my throat.
When they came they found
our arms strewn around the floor
like broken toys.
We both were crying.

5

You stick. Somewhere in a cellar of my mind,
you stick. Fruit spoke to you
before it spoke to me. Apples cried
when you peeled them.
Tangerines jabbered in Japanese.
You stared into an oyster
& sucked out God.
You were the hollow man,
with Milton entering your left foot.

6

My first husband!—God—
you've become an abstraction,
a kind of Idea. I can't even hear

your voice any more. Only the black hair
curled on your belly makes you real—
I draw black curls on all the men I write.
I don't even look anymore.

7

I thought of you in Istanbul.
Your Byzantine face,
thin lips & hollow cheeks,
the fanatical melting brown eyes.
In Hagia Sophia they're stripping down
the moslem plaster
to find mosaics underneath.
The pieces fit in place.
You'd have been a Saint.

8

I'm good at interiors.
Gossip, sharpening edges, kitchen poems—
& have no luck at all with maps.
It's because of being a woman
& having everything inside.
I decorated the cave,
hung it with animal skins & woolens,
such soft floors,
that when you fell
you thought you fell on me.
You had a perfect sense of bearings
to the end,
were always pointing North.

9

Flying you home—
good Christ—flying you home,
you were terrified.
You held my hand, I held
my father's hand & he
filched pills from the psychiatrist
who'd come along for you.
The psychiatrist was 26 & scared.
He hoped I'd keep you calm.
& so we flew.
Hand in hand in hand in hand we flew.

Narcissus, Photographer

> *". . . a frozen memory, like any photo,*
> *where nothing is missing, not even,*
> *and especially, nothingness. . ."*
> —*Julio Cortázar, "Blow Up"*

Mirror-mad,
he photographed reflections:
sunstorms in puddles,
cities in canals,

double portraits framed
in sunglasses,
the fat phantoms who dance
on the flanks of cars.

Nothing caught his eye
unless it bent
or glistered
over something else.

He trapped clouds in bottles
the way kids
trap grasshoppers.
Then one misty day

he was stopped
by the windshield.
Behind him,
an avenue of trees,

before him,
the mirror of that scene.
He seemed to enter
what, in fact, he left.

Flower Eaters

"Browning wrote to his friend that he would sometimes bite flowers and leaves to bits 'in an impatience at being unable to possess myself of them thoroughly, to see them quite, to satiate myself with their scent.'"

Browning, you make me want
a nineteenth-century mouth
(greater, I mean, than the sum
of its devourings)
because I am trying, trying
to sidle the iris between slick teeth,
to tongue the crocuses and roses—
but it's no use.
They've cut off my honey.
Does my tongue no longer love me?
(Did it ever?)
No longer mother me?
Its hunger runs on, runs on.
Its anger!
Meanwhile you're gorging on pink petals
& waxy white pistils
(and the kids protest that they've discovered flowers!)
& I sit here wondering:
how many have devoured the world?
how much remains?
Despite the various subtle forms of lockjaw
(despite this tongue so stubbornly stuck in my cheek),
can poetry still enter through the mouth?

Nowadays, who can afford
a nineteenth-century mouth?
Roethke arrived and the greenhouse revolted.
New blooms fought up like Robespierres.
Orchids were "adder-mouthed,"
the roses appalling,
the cyclamen suddenly sneaky.
Old weed-puller, old fearer.
You tried to breathe the dirt.
(It filled your mouth.)
You never died,
you just stopped hungering.
Sylvia kept bees & they kept her
(thinking to learn the honey-sucking secrets).
Flowers were animal mouths, devourers
growing up towards a father who blazed like the sun.
In the end, your daughter fled
to the heart of the hive.

Browning, you wouldn't believe it.
The flowers have had us.
I try to take the roses with my teeth.
I suck for honey & gulp air.
Dear Browning, put on your hat,
your Victorian hat.
Put on your mouth, your gestures.
Put a flower in your mouth.
Only a hundred years and yet,
we don't eat flowers any more.
It works
the other way around.

You Operate

You operate on the afternoon
You perform open heart surgery
on the ghosts
of your suicidal friends

You divorce your parents
before you have time
to be born

You kick out your wife & child
You tell your girlfriend
to go screw herself

This is the solitude you wanted
The silence
is stitching you up
you write

Books

*"The universe (which others call
the library) . . ."*
                    —Jorge Luis Borges

Books which are stitched up the center with coarse white
thread
Books on the beach with sunglass-colored pages
Books about food with pictures of weeping grapefruits
Books about baking bread with browned corners
Books about long-haired Frenchmen with uncut pages
Books of erotic engravings with pages that stick
Books about inns whose stars have sputtered out
Books of illuminations surrounded by darkness
Books with blank pages & printed margins
Books with fanatical footnotes in no-point type
Books with book lice
Books with rice-paper pastings
Books with book fungus blooming over their pages
Books with pages of skin with flesh-colored bindings
Books by men in love with the letter O
Books which smell of earth whose pages turn

The Book

I float down the spiral stairs
of the old apartment.
At the dining room table sit
my six ex-analysts, two brokers,
& five professors,
considering my book.
They dip the pages of the manuscript in water,
to see if it will last.

From where I watch, the sheets look blank.

They discuss my sexual hang-ups.
Why do I write about women
when, after all, they're men?
They enumerate my debts, losses,
& the lies I've told; the red lights
I have passed, the men I've kissed.

They examine a lock of my hair for bleach.

Finally, muttering, they rise & yawn in chorus.
They decide to repossess my typewriter, my legs,
my Phi Beta Kappa key, one breast,
any children I may have,
& my espresso machine.

My book, of course, is through.
Already the pages have dissolved like toilet paper.

I wake up with the bed
still on the wrong side of the dream.
My legs are scattered through the streets
like pick-up sticks.
Crawling on stumps, crawling
in the spittle & dog shit,
I bitterly accuse the City
& bitterly accuse myself.

How could I not have known
that the book was on the wrong side
of the dream?
How could I
have walked into it?

Where It Begins

The corruption begins with the eyes,
the page, the hunger.
It hangs on the first hook
of the first comma.

The mouth shuts & opens.
Newspapers are there & nursery rhymes.
Readers, lovers dangle
like Cassius, Brutus
from Satan's teeth.

The corruption begins with the mouth,
the tongue, the wanting.
The first poem in the world
is *I want to eat.*

The breast is the screen
of the dream;
no hungry poet
can ever be content
with two.

The corruption begins with the breasts,
the cunt, the navel.
It begins with wanting love
from strangers.

The breasts are two blind animals
with painted eyes.

The cunt is a furry deaf mute
speaking a red tongue.
The tongue is hunger.

The corruption begins with the curled snail
of the baby.
It begins with the white flood
of love on pages.

It begins with emptiness
where love begins.
It begins with love
where emptiness
begins.